BOOKS

GOLF
100 ways to improve your game

TENNIS
Basic Techniques and Tactics

PHOTOGRAPHY
Using a 35mm camera

YOGA
The happy way to live

JUDO
The practical way

MOTORCYCLES
Maintain your own machine

SWIMMING
Learning, training, competing

MOTORCARS
Maintenance and minor repairs

FIRST AID
And emergency care

HOME MOVIES
Make and project your own films

COOKERY
Skills of French cuisine

© Chancerel 1976
    English language edition
© Chancerel Publishers Ltd. 1977

All rights reserved. No part of this publication may be reproduced, recorded, transmitted or stored in any retrieval system, in any form whatsoever, without the written permission of the copyright holder.
This edition is not for sale in the USA.
Chancerel Publishers Ltd.,
40 Tavistock Street,
London WC2E 7PB.
ISBN 0-905703-06-5
Photoset in Great Britain
Printed in Italy

SWIMMING
Learning, Training, Competing

Charlie Wilson

Drawings by J. Arbeau

Brian Brinkley, MBE

The greatest British swimmer of this decade.
Born in 1953 in Peterborough, England. Swam for Peterborough Swimming Club until he was 16½.
"Never in the age-group rat race, I was always on the edge of the swimming scene."
Burst into National swimming in 1971 after joining Charlie Wilson's Modernian Swimming Club, in Bedford. Since 1971 he has won 49 British titles. He is a Commonwealth gold, silver and bronze medallist over six events; a European silver medallist and a silver medallist in the World Championships 1975.
Swam in 1972 and 1976 Olympic Games, winning a bronze medal in 1976.
Great Britain team captain 1974 to 1976.
In January 1976 he was awarded the MBE for services to sport.
Main events: 200m Butterfly and 200m and 400m Freestyle.

It's a marvellous feeling to speed through water. There's such a sense of power in driving forward with your own strength and skill, the water surging past your face. And that's the challenge this book offers in easy steps: learn to swim — really well.

It also features something unusual in books about swimming; it emphasises and demonstrates the role of the coach. And to be a good swimmer you must have a good teacher.

We all need to succeed. We all need to be shown how. In these simple, direct picture strips — and some unusual word pictures as well — Charlie Wilson makes success straightforward and uncomplicated. He and this book can help you reach the top.

Brian Brinkley, MBE

Contents

INTO THE WATER	9
The swim babes	10
Equipment	10
Necessary precautions	12
You can't swim without water	12
Breathing when swimming	13
Into the water	13
Glide position	15
Push and glide	15

YOUR FIRST STROKES	17
Floating on your back	18
Take a breath through your mouth	18
The tunnel game	19
A seven metre glide	19
Front crawl arm action	20
Breathe both sides	20
Finally — learn to dive	22
Digestion and drowning	22
Water, fat and calories	23
The world of sport	23
Living, eating and swimming	25
A swimmer's diet	25

STYLES FOR EVERYONE	27
Front crawl	28
Pull and push backwards — not up and down	28
The rolling drill	29
From rolling drill to Front crawl	29
Variety of timing	30
The feel of the water	30
Avoid lateral movement	32
High elbows	32
Underwater study	33
Leg action	33
Progress with your leg kick	35
Arms only	35
Pull and push	36
Backstroke — arms together	36
Left, right, left	38
Backstroke — arm technique	38
A foot like a pigeon's wing	39
Backstroke timing	39
Breaststroke	40
Old and new techniques	40
The water wall	41
No prayers please!	41
Arm and leg action	42
Mark Spitz' swimming	42
The dolphin undulation	44
The dolphin kick with a board	44
Arms are important	45
Racing start: an essential detail	45
The start from a starting block	46
The grab start	46
Similarities between starts	48
Head position	48
Underwater glide	49
The start with no fear problems	49
Tumble turns	50
The impossible tumble turn	50
Backstroke turns	52
Another method of learning	52
Walking babes or baby pianists?	53

TRAINING AND COMPETITION 55
The feel of the water 56
Distance per stroke 56
15 Metres in 50 years 57
15 Kilometres a day 57
Planning your programme 58
Be supple 58
Not too bulky 60
Be comfortable 60
Specifics — quality resistance training 61
Muscle training 61
Resistance training in water 63
Kevin Berry's drogue 63
Oxygen 64
Potatoes — athlete's food 64
The steak myth dies 65
Conquering nerves 65
Race tactics 67
Do the unexpected — within reason! 67
Bilateral breathing 68

MAKING HISTORY 71
The thousand year old crawl 72
Japanese first 72
The beginning of the modern era 74
Tarzan beaten by a woman 74
1500 metres — minute by minute 75
Birth of Butterfly 75

DERIVED ACTIVITIES 77
Try the diving board 78
Straight, tucked, piked 78
Variety in diving 79
Entry: beware of landing flat 79
Gymnastics for divers 81
A man's game 81
Water polo 82
Dribble, pass and shoot 82
A game of many facets 84
A sport for women 84
Figures and stunts 85
Swimming for all ages 85
Sub aqua 86
Long distance swimming 86
Swimming — new horizons 87

GREAT NAMES IN SWIMMING HISTORY 88
SWIMMING TERMS 89
SWIMMING ORGANISATIONS 89
BIOGRAPHY 90
PHOTOGRAPHS 91

Into the water

In order to swim, you must enter a different element — water. It feels strange at first and it can be a frightening experience for some people. So remember never to force beginners into swimming against their wills. Never ridicule the fear of water — it's all too real. Time spent helping beginners to overcome initial hesitation pays off in later progress.

The swim babes

Equipment

Necessary precautions

You can't swim without water

Breathing when swimming

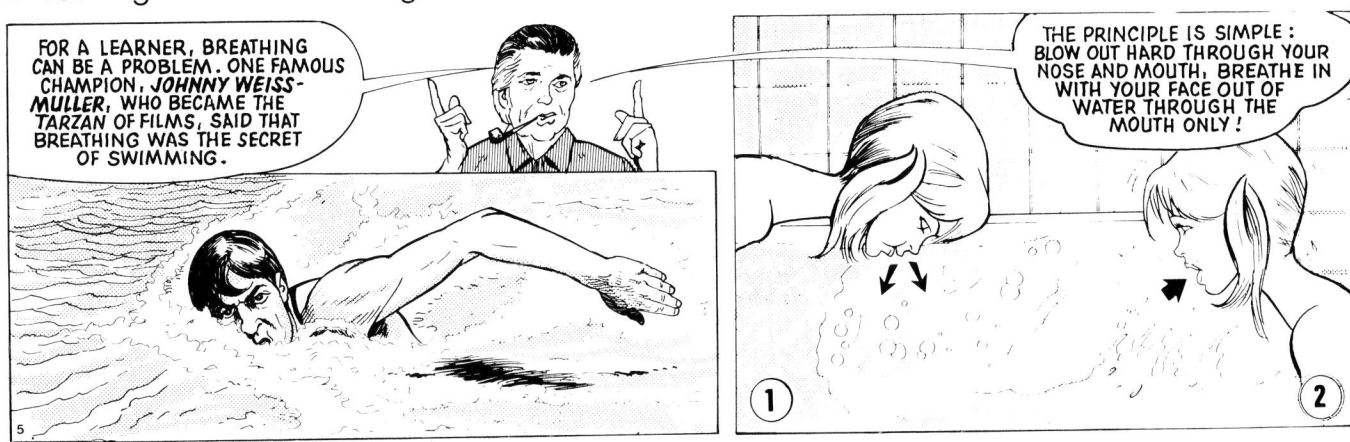

Into the water

Glide position

Push and glide

Your first strokes

When you are used to the water you must learn how to move through it — to swim the basic strokes. This requires a certain degree of fitness, which is good for anyone. Taken one step further, training implies a new life-style, which is essential for success in competitions.

Floating on your back

Take a breath through your mouth

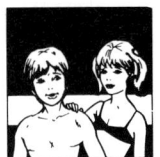

The tunnel game

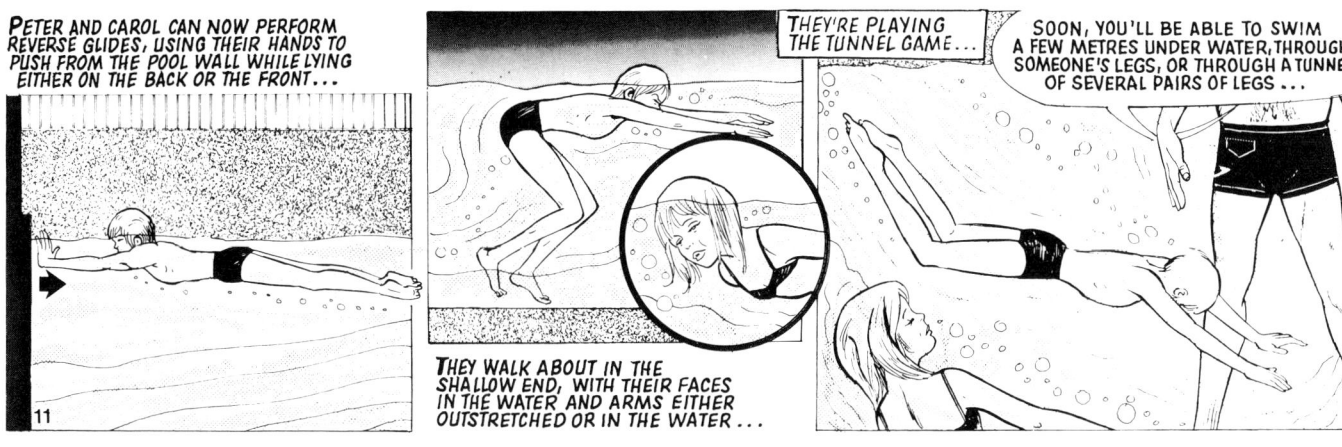

A seven metre glide

Front crawl arm action

Breathe both sides

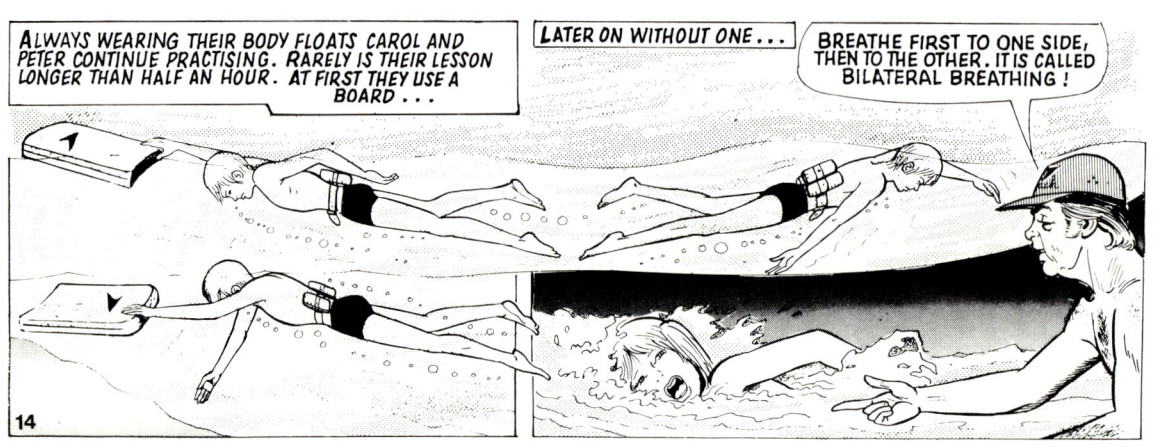

Finally — learn to dive

Digestion and drowning

Water, fat and calories

The world of sport

Living, eating and swimming

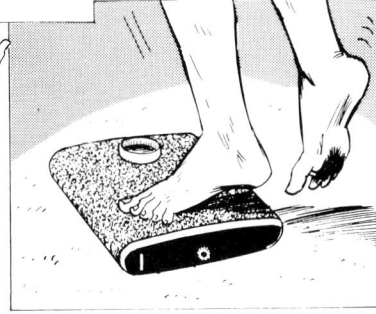

19. Gradually, as they do more and more swimming, Peter and Carol get used to a well regulated daily schedule. They go to bed early to allow complete recovery. They need 9-10 hours sleep...

There's a saying..."We are what we eat." In order to prevent accumulative fatigue from swimming lessons and schooling, they eat plenty of good food in a well-balanced diet...

The twins train regularly, but if they become excessively tired, or if they lose weight or appetite, their parents, in consultation with their coach, insist on rest.

A swimmer's diet

20. A swimmer eats as much as he wants. According to Dr. Counsilman, he needs a pint of milk, meat or fish, two eggs, cereals, bread or potatoes, sugar, raw salad, fruit or vegetable juice and cooked vegetables every day...

On race days he should eat easily digested foods which rapidly release their energy. Therefore, the rule is light foods, avoiding too much meat, fats and milk. Replace these with carbohydrates— bread, potatoes and cooked vegetables...

Neither food nor living principles make champions, but they help to improve performance. Champions are made by the careful and intelligent application of hard training!

Styles for everyone

There are as many different ways of swimming as there are individuals in the water. But careful study has proved that some styles are more effective than others when it comes to moving people through water. This has enabled competitions to be standardised, using the principle strokes — Back crawl, Breaststroke, Butterfly and Front crawl. Freestyle is nowadays limited to Front crawl, which is by far the fastest stroke yet devised.

Front crawl

Pull and push backwards — not up and down

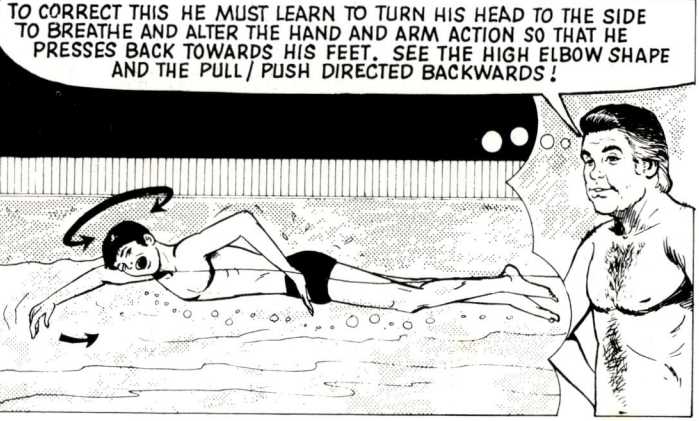

The rolling drill

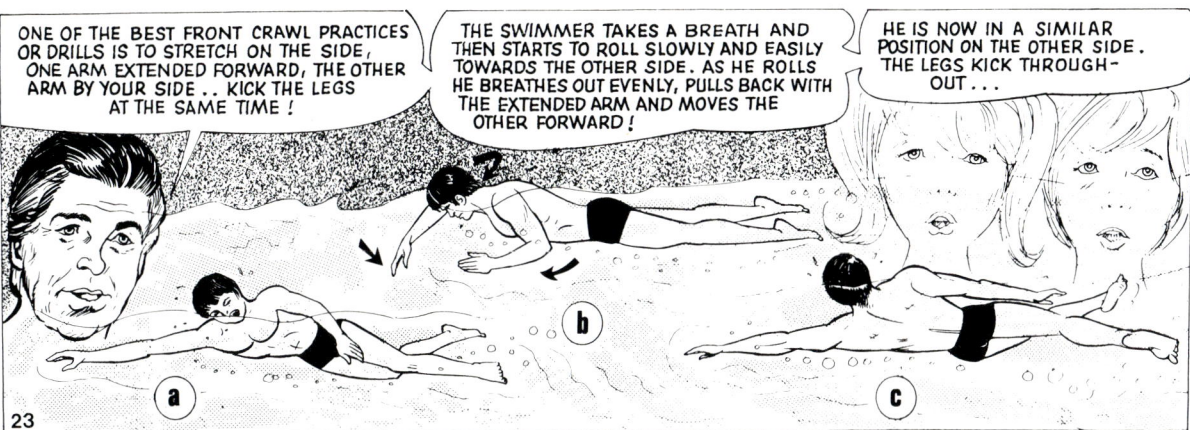

ONE OF THE BEST FRONT CRAWL PRACTICES OR DRILLS IS TO STRETCH ON THE SIDE, ONE ARM EXTENDED FORWARD, THE OTHER ARM BY YOUR SIDE .. KICK THE LEGS AT THE SAME TIME!

THE SWIMMER TAKES A BREATH AND THEN STARTS TO ROLL SLOWLY AND EASILY TOWARDS THE OTHER SIDE. AS HE ROLLS HE BREATHES OUT EVENLY, PULLS BACK WITH THE EXTENDED ARM AND MOVES THE OTHER FORWARD!

HE IS NOW IN A SIMILAR POSITION ON THE OTHER SIDE. THE LEGS KICK THROUGHOUT...

THIS EXERCISE TEACHES THE SWIMMER HOW TO TURN ON THE LONG AXIS OF THE BODY (LIKE A PIG ON A SPIT) HOW TO CONTROL HIS BREATHING .. HOW TO PULL AND PUSH BACKWARDS.. AND HOW TO KEEP THE LEG ACTION GOING THROUGHOUT THE STROKE...

From rolling drill to Front crawl

ONCE THE ROLLING DRILL HAS BEEN LEARNED WELL, IT IS PRACTISED WITH SLIGHT MODIFICATIONS. THE ARM LYING ALONG THE SIDE IS NOW BROUGHT FORWARD OUT OF THE WATER INSTEAD OF UNDERNEATH. THE BREATH IS STILL TAKEN ON BOTH SIDES...

FINAL STEP: THE SWIMMER NOW CHANGES HIS POSITION WITHOUT TURNING COMPLETELY ON TO HIS SIDE.. THERE'S NO PAUSE IN THE MOVEMENT AND HE BREATHES ON ONE SIDE ONLY... HE'S MADE IT!

HURRAH! HE'S A FRONT CRAWLER!

Variety of timing

The feel of the water

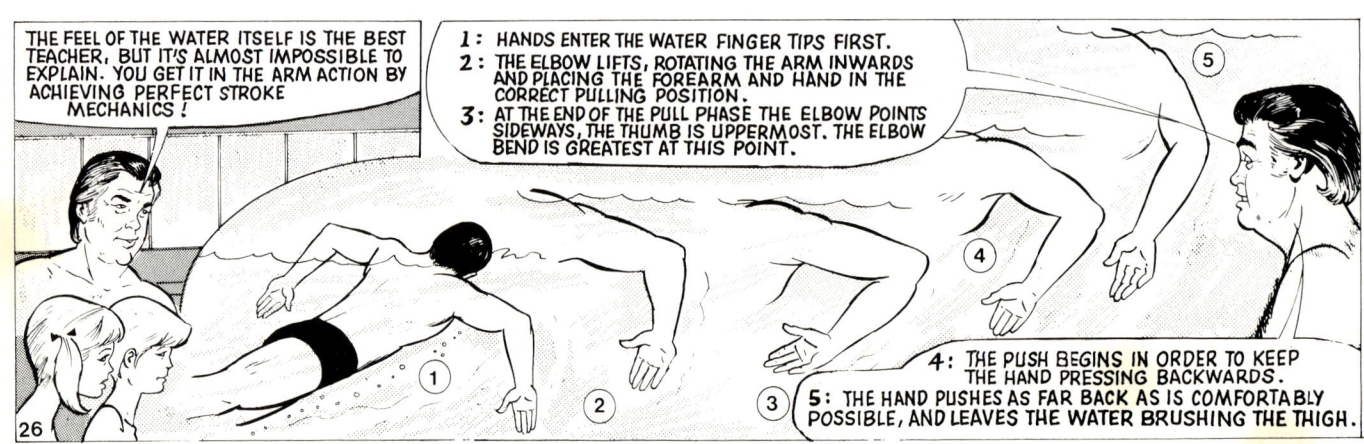

Avoid lateral movement

High elbows

Underwater study

29

The twins are enthralled by the underwater view...

MR WOODS, DO YOU OFTEN CONTROL TRAINING FROM HERE?

ACCORDING TO *DR COUNSILMAN*, WHO BROUGHT NEW CONCEPTS INTO SWIMMING TRAINING THROUGH HIS WORK AT INDIANA UNIVERSITY, THIS ASPECT OF TRAINING IS GOOD FOR TECHNIQUE WORK AT THE BEGINNING OF THE SEASON. AFTER THAT, UNDERWATER VIEWING AND FILMING HAS LIMITED VALUE...

NORMAL OBSERVATION OF STROKE CANNOT DETECT STROKE MECHANICS ACCURATELY. UNDERWATER VIEWING REMEDIES THIS. A SWIMMER IS LIKE AN ICEBERG—THE BULK AND THE VITAL PART IS UNDERWATER. UNFORTUNATELY FEW POOLS ARE EQUIPPED FOR UNDERWATER OBSERVATION...

Leg action

30

PETER AND CAROL, THIS IS PAUL, A TOP CLASS FREESTYLER...

MANY COACHES ASSERT THAT *KICKING* DOESN'T HELP PROPULSION, IT SIMPLY BALANCES THE ARM ACTION. OTHERS, MAYBE JUST AS COMPETENT, ARE JUST AS SURE THAT THE KICK *DOES* ADD PROPULSION. SOME SWIMMERS TRAVEL PRETTY FAST USING LEGS ONLY!

LET'S FORGET THE ARGUMENT. JUST REMEMBER THAT WHEN THE ARMS START PULLING, THE LEGS ARE ESSENTIALLY BALANCING AND STABILISING. IN THE WORDS OF *FORBES CARLILE*, THE FAMOUS AUSTRALIAN COACH, THE KICK SHOULD NEVER CONTROL THE ARM ACTION...

Progress with your leg kick

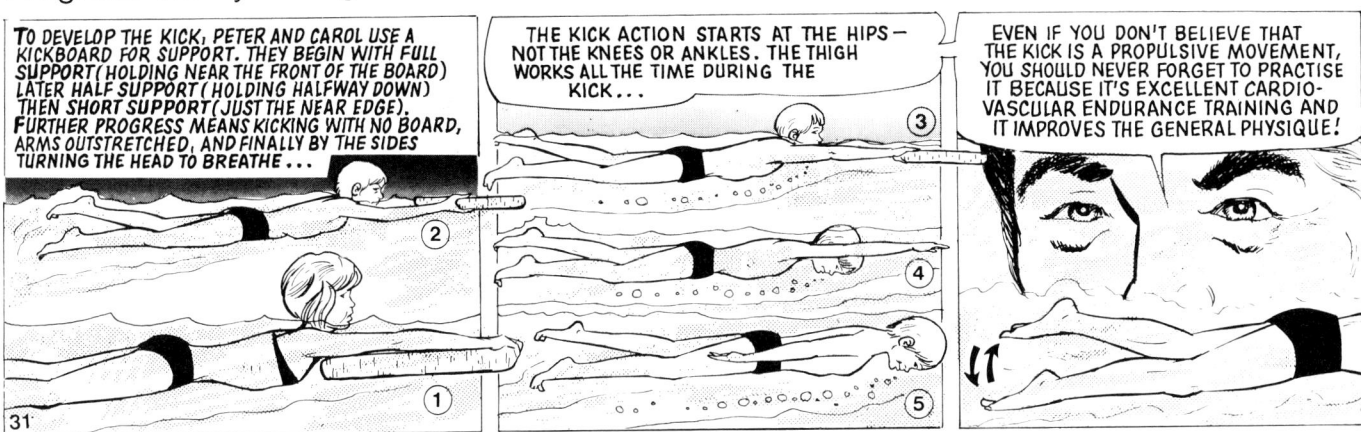

Arms only

Pull and push

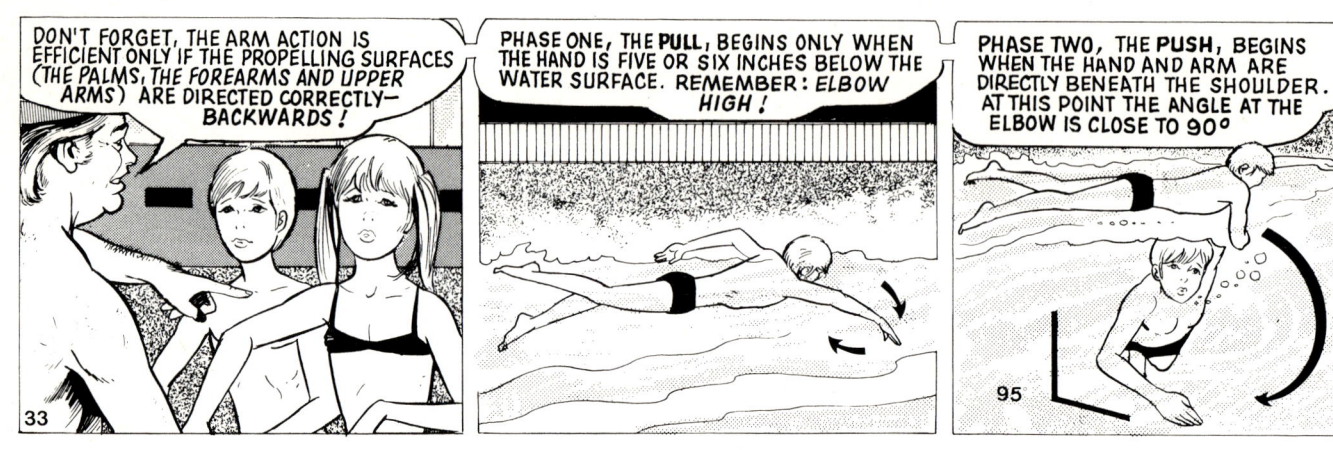

Backstroke — arms together

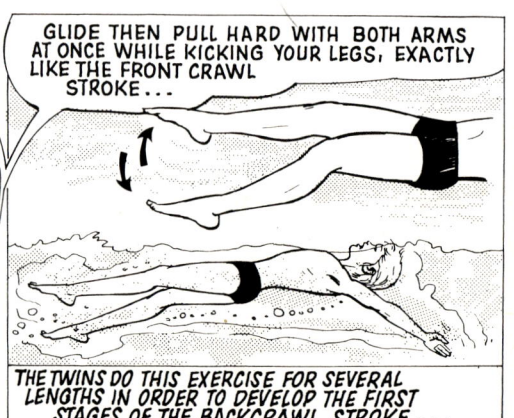

Left, right, left

Backstroke — arm technique

A foot like a pigeon's wing

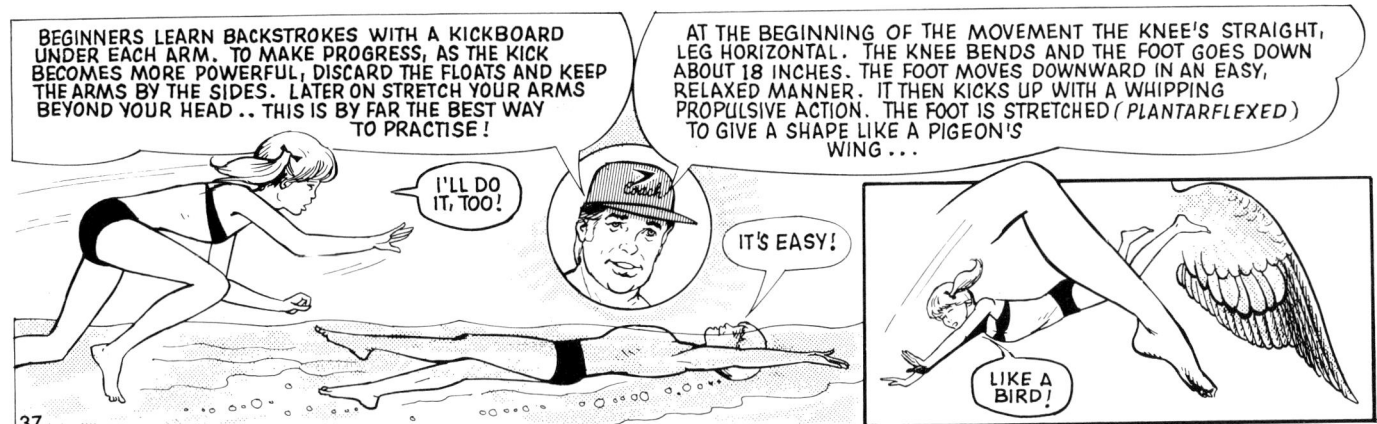

Backstroke timing

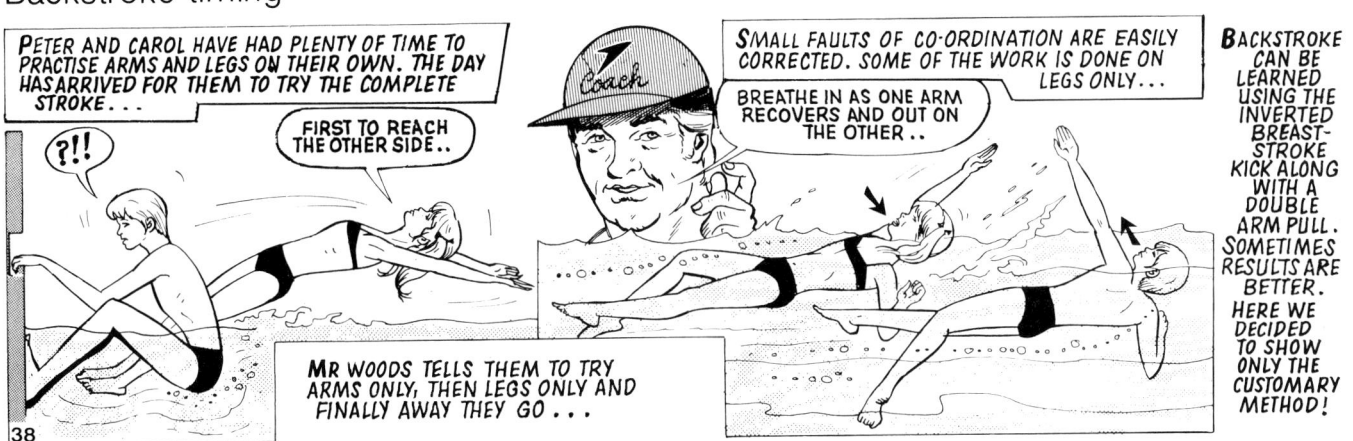

Breaststroke

Old and new techniques

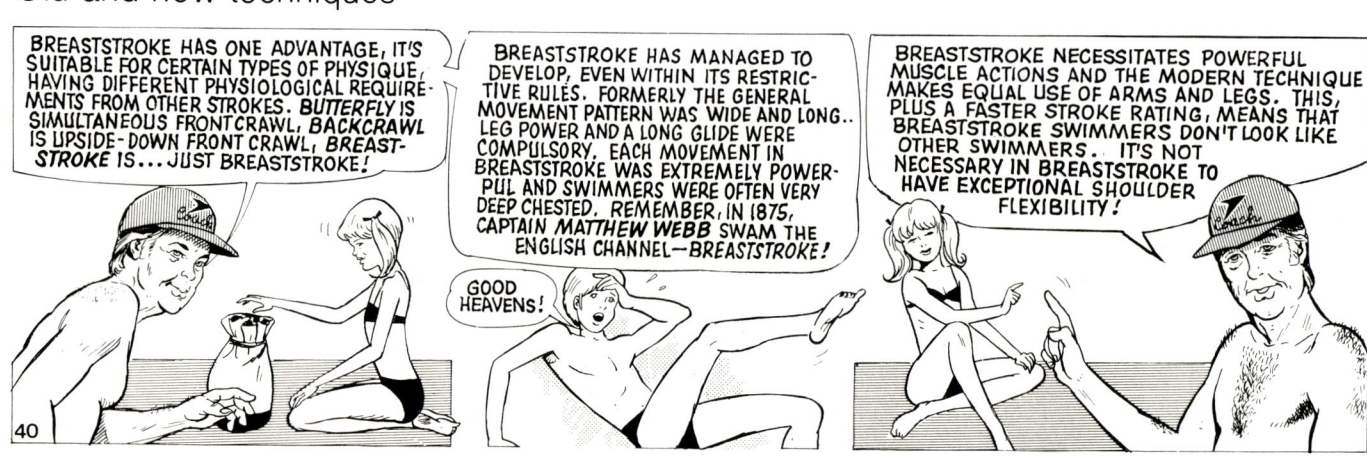

The water wall

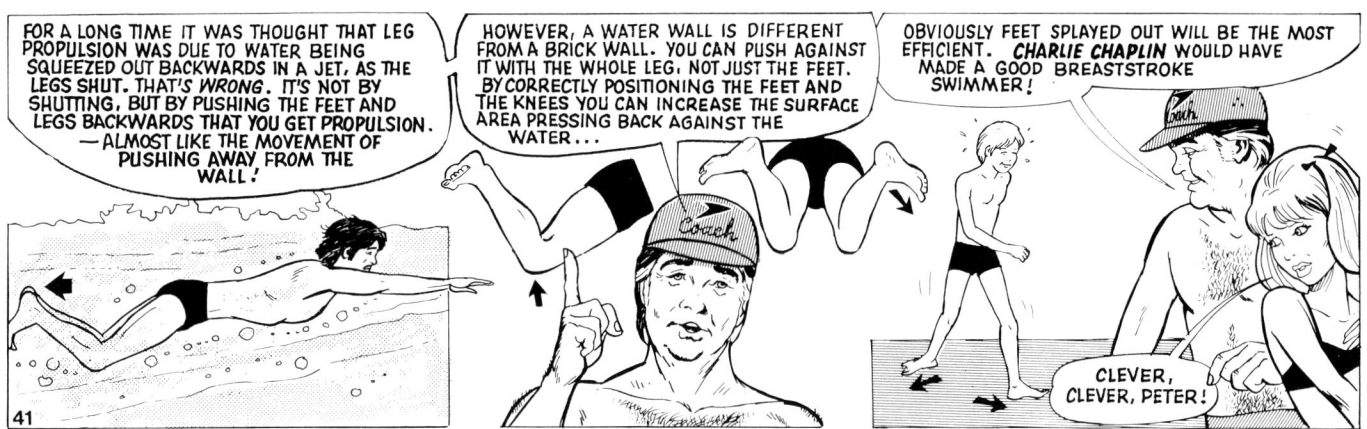

No prayers please!

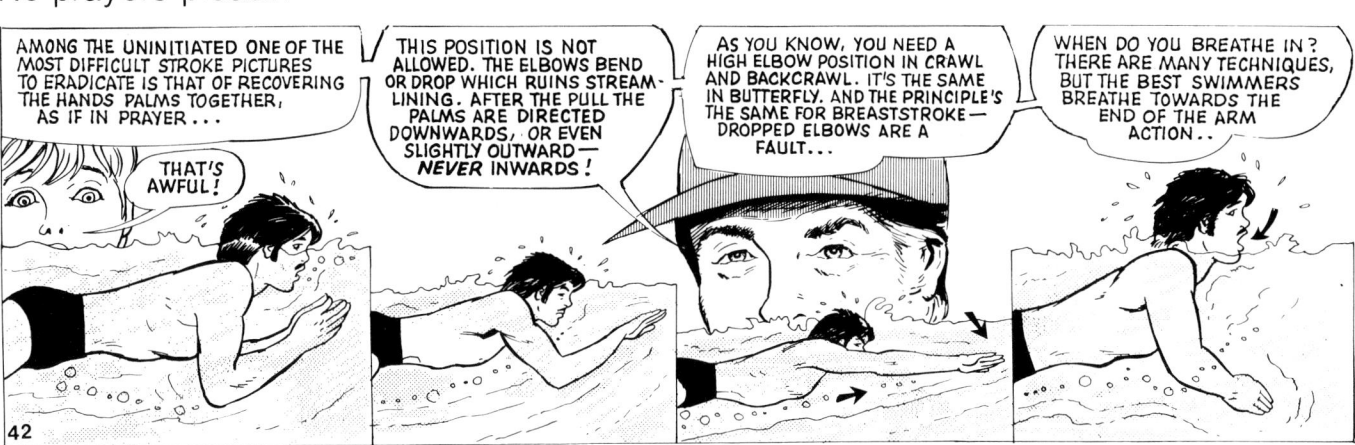

Arm and leg action

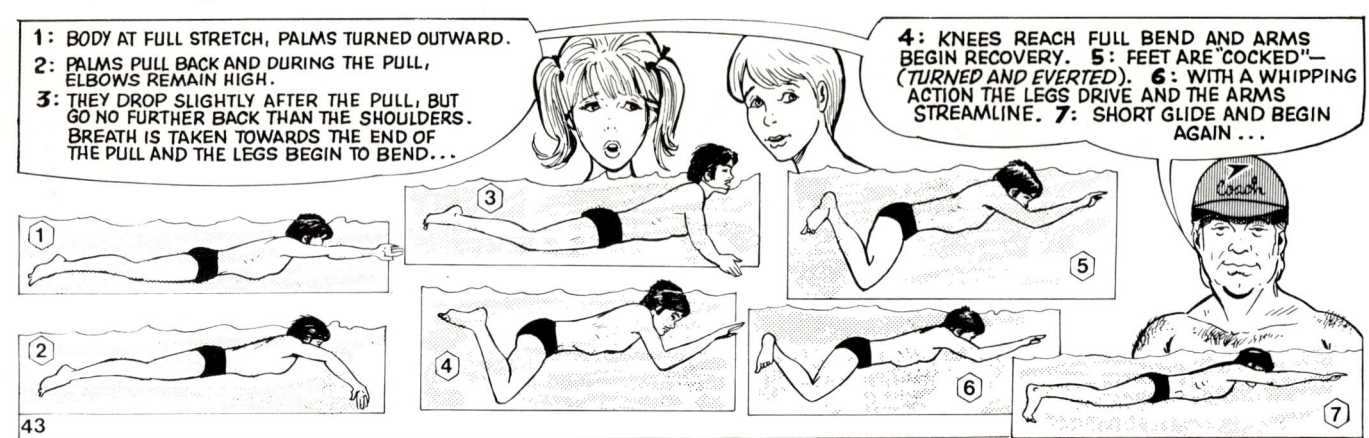

Mark Spitz' swimming

The dolphin undulation

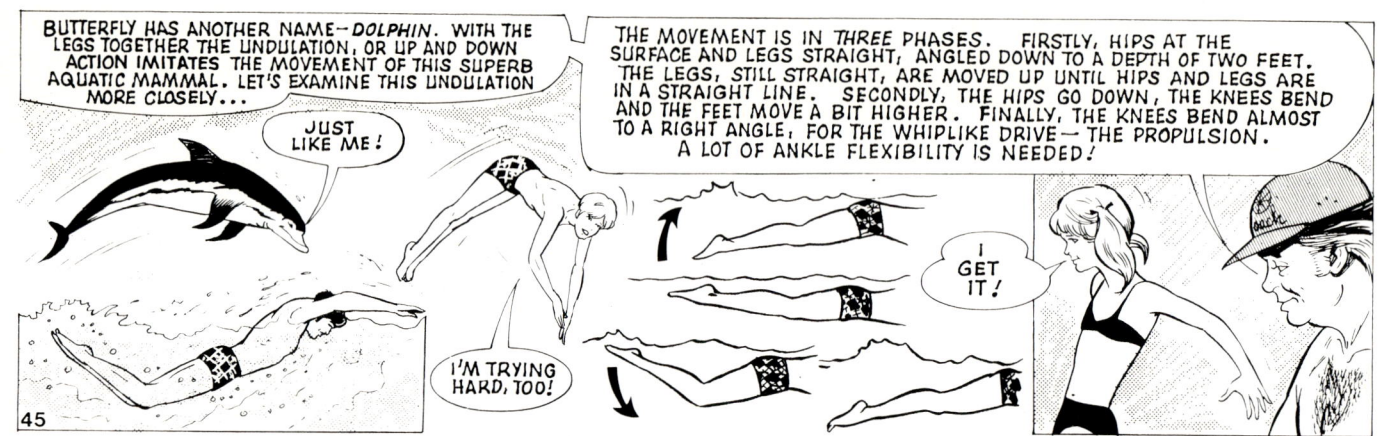

The dolphin kick with a board

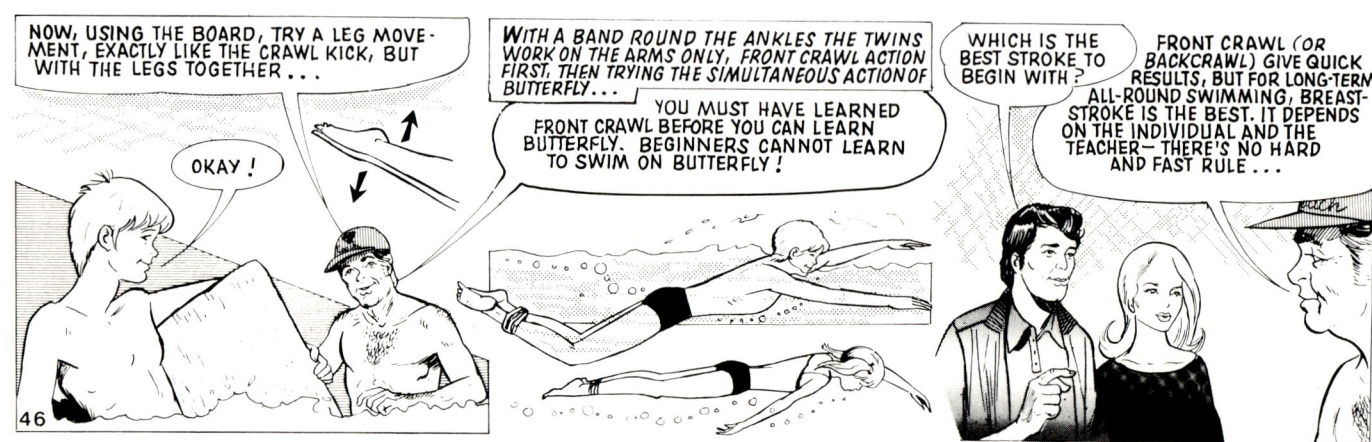

Arms are important

Racing start: an essential detail

The start from a starting block

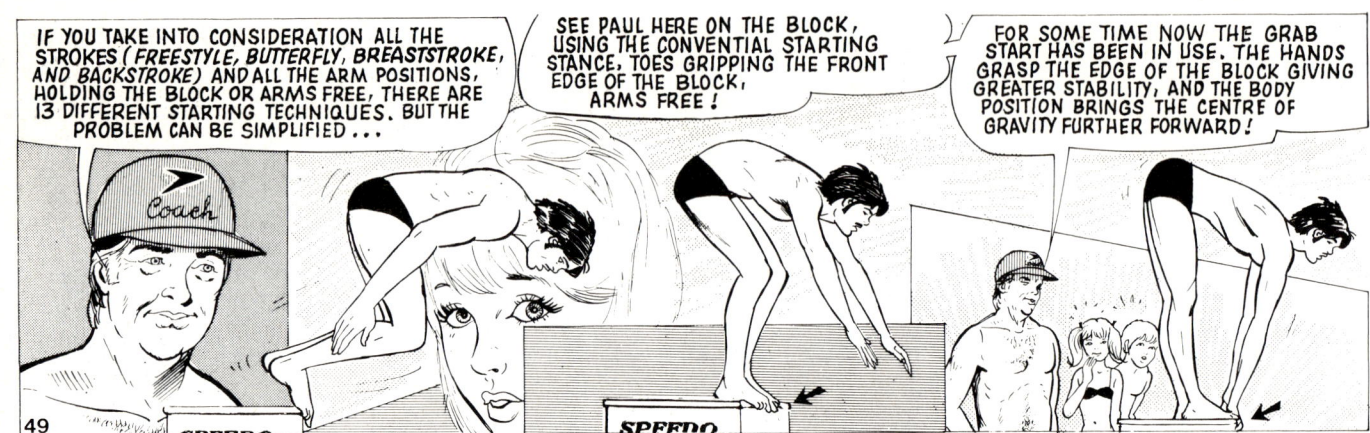

The grab start

Similarities between starts

Head position

Underwater glide

The start with no fear problems

Tumble turns

The impossible tumble turn

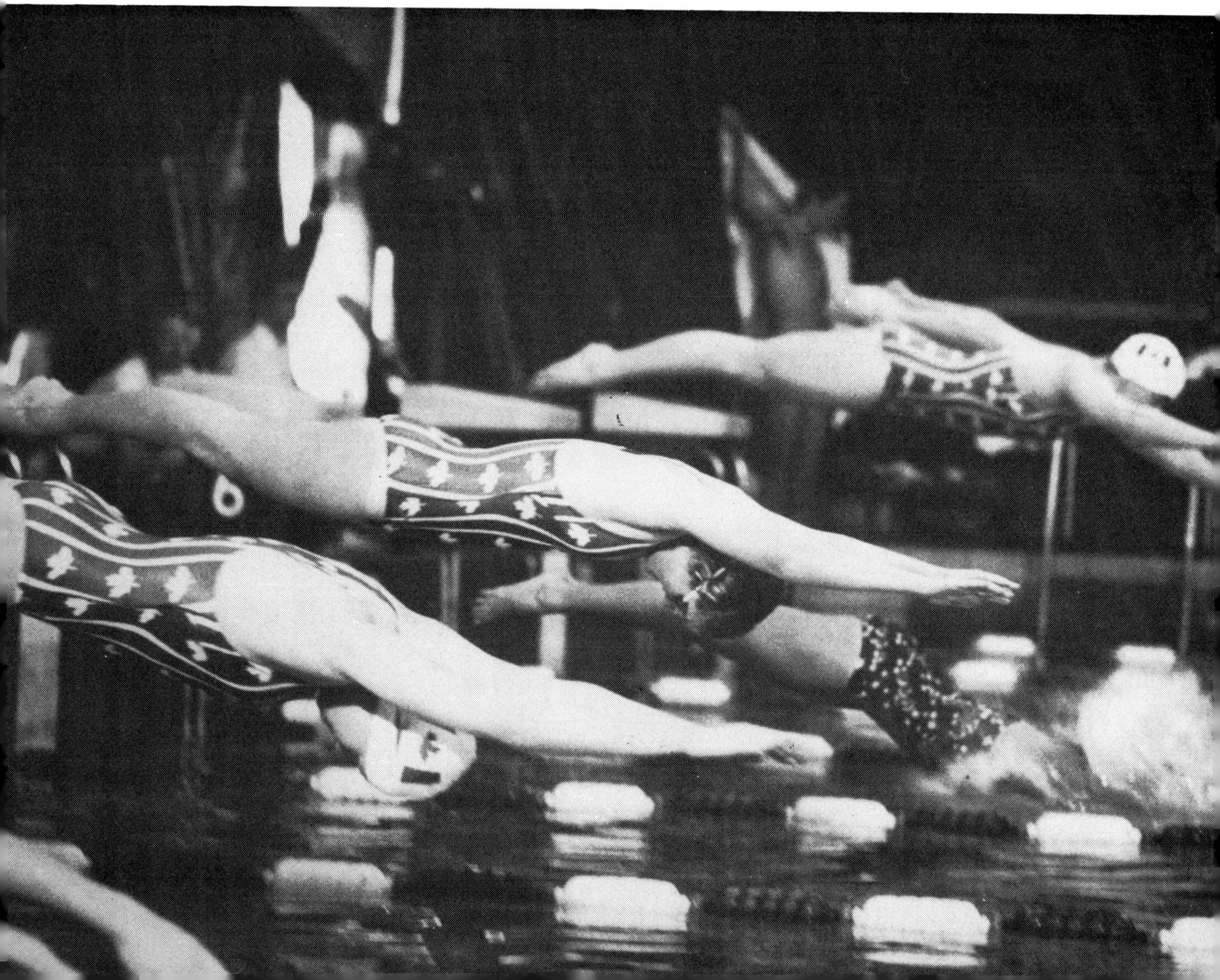

Backstroke turns

Another method of learning

Walking-babes or baby pianists?

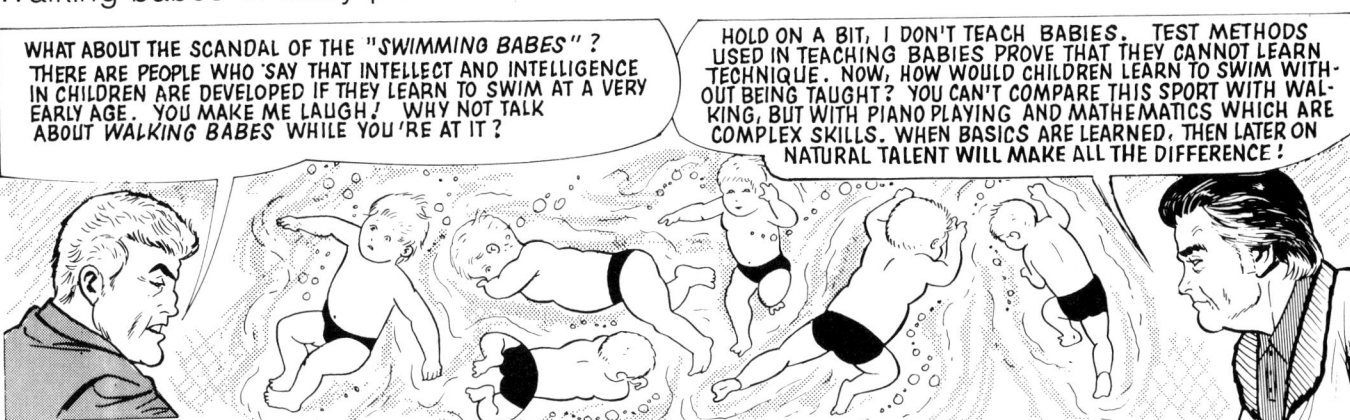

Training and competition

You have learned the four strokes and all about starts and turns. That means it's time to think about competitions. From school to the Olympic Games competitions are the objectives of coaches and serious swimmers alike. Here you have the chance to study the most important features of the latest coaching programmes, which include bilateral breathing, physique, oxygen uptake and diet. Did you know that "the steak for strength" theory was a myth?

The feel of the water

Distance per stroke

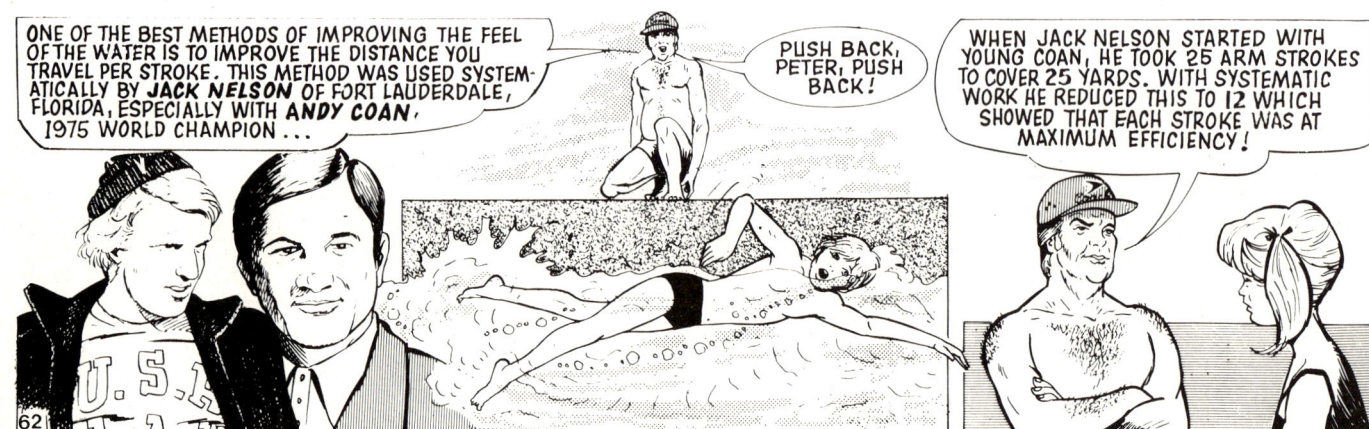

15 Metres in 50 years

15 Kilometres a day

Planning your programme

Be supple

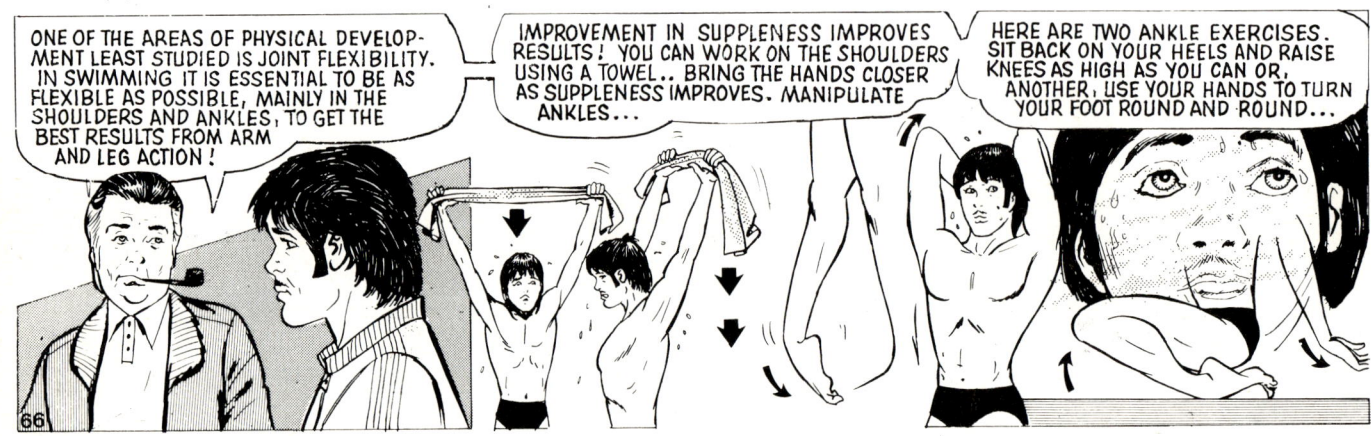

Not too bulky

Be comfortable

Specifics — quality resistance training

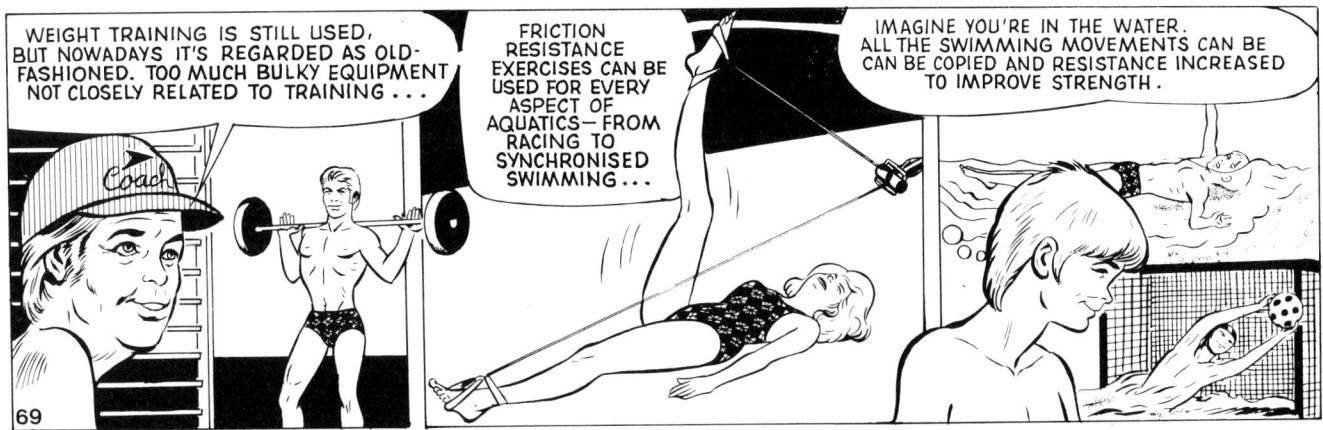

Muscle training

Resistance training in water

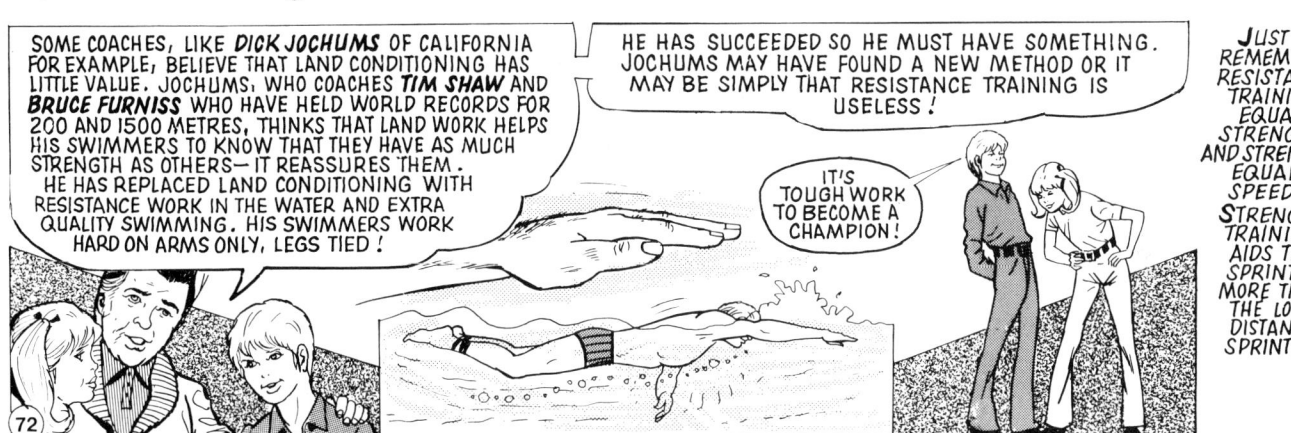

Kevin Berry's drogue

Oxygen

Potatoes — athlete's food

The steak myth dies

Conquering nerves

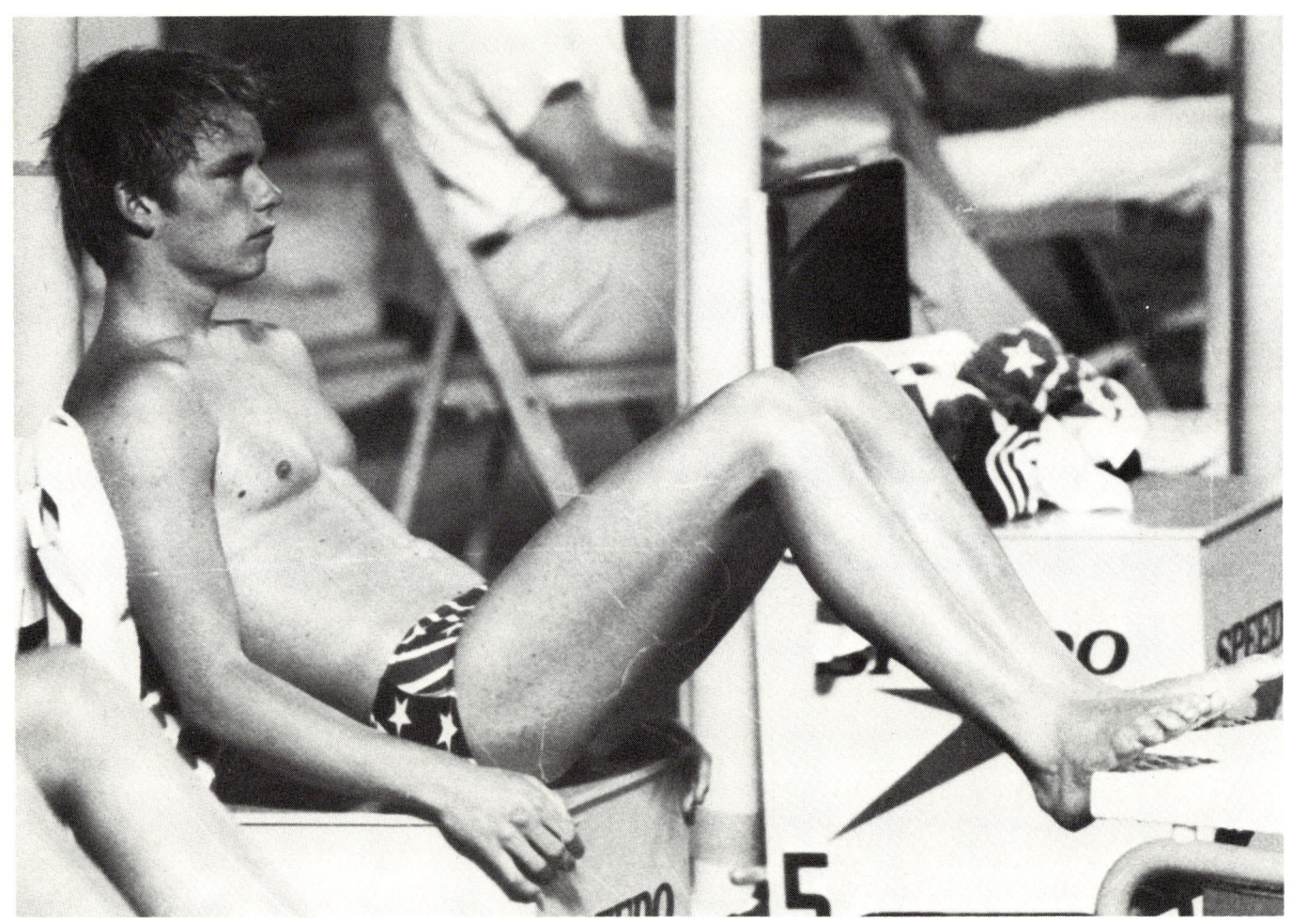

Race tactics

Do the unexpected — within reason!

Bilateral breathing

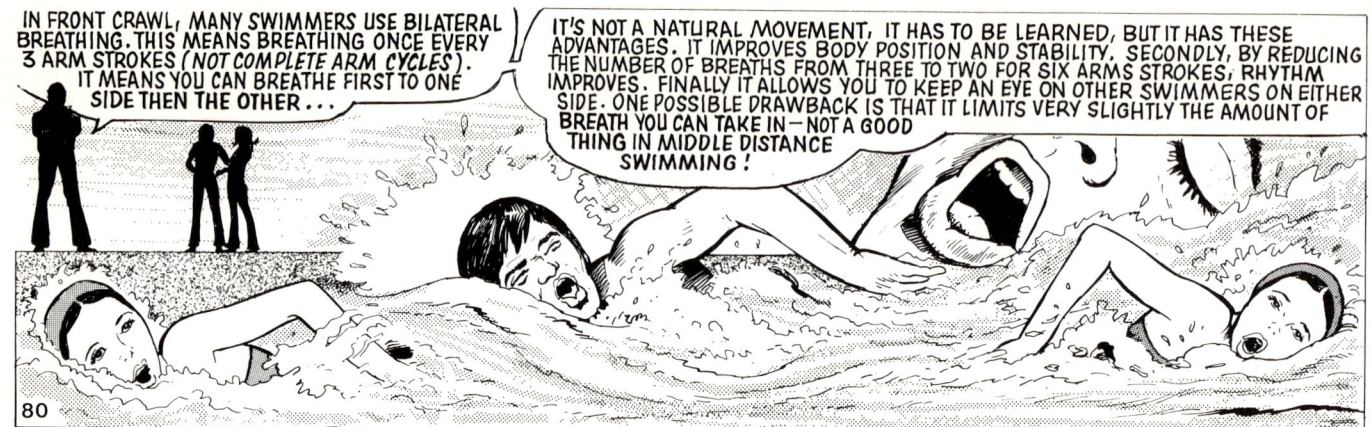

Making history

Competitive swimming may have a relatively short history, but it is now the fastest developing sport in the world. The proof of that lies in the speed with which impossible records have been broken and broken again. In 1976 a 17-year old girl swam the 100 metres Freestyle nearly three seconds faster than that famous swimming and screen star of the 1930's, Johnny Weissmuller, alias Tarzan. And other young girls and boys will go faster yet, you can be sure. In the water even history is accelerating.

The thousand year old crawl

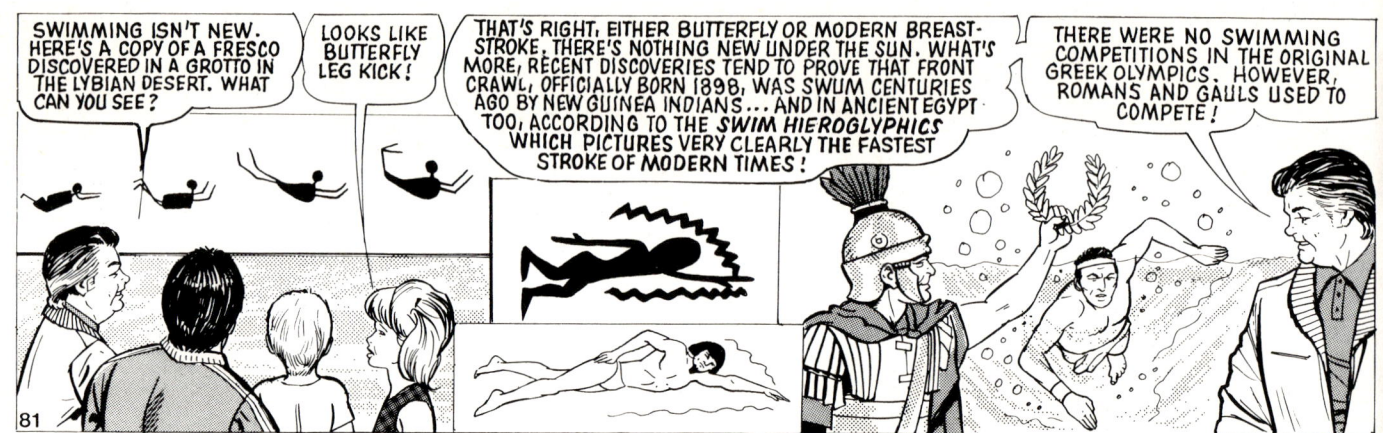

Japanese first

The beginning of the modern era

Tarzan beaten by a woman

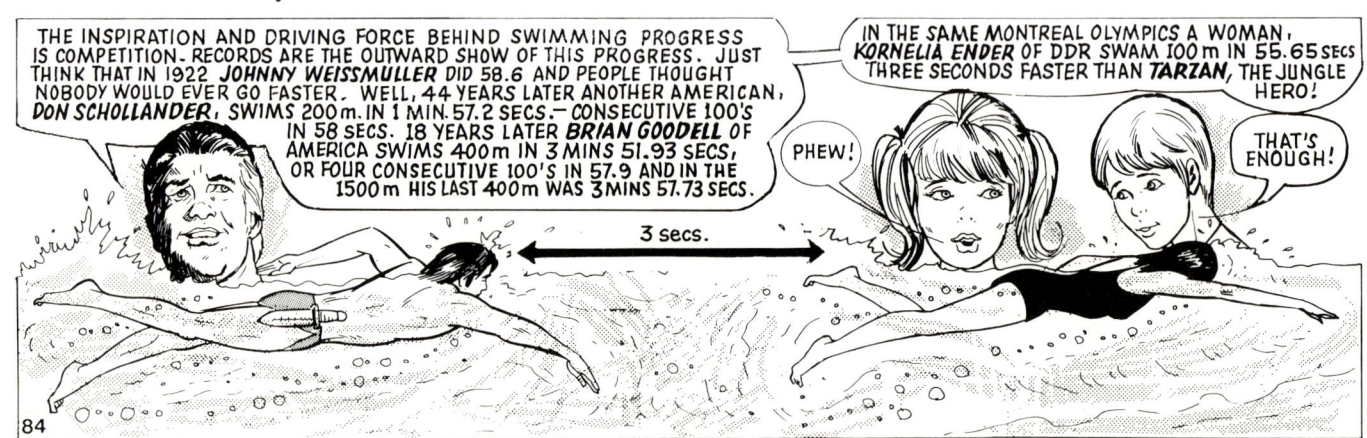

1500 metres — minute by minute

Birth of Butterfly

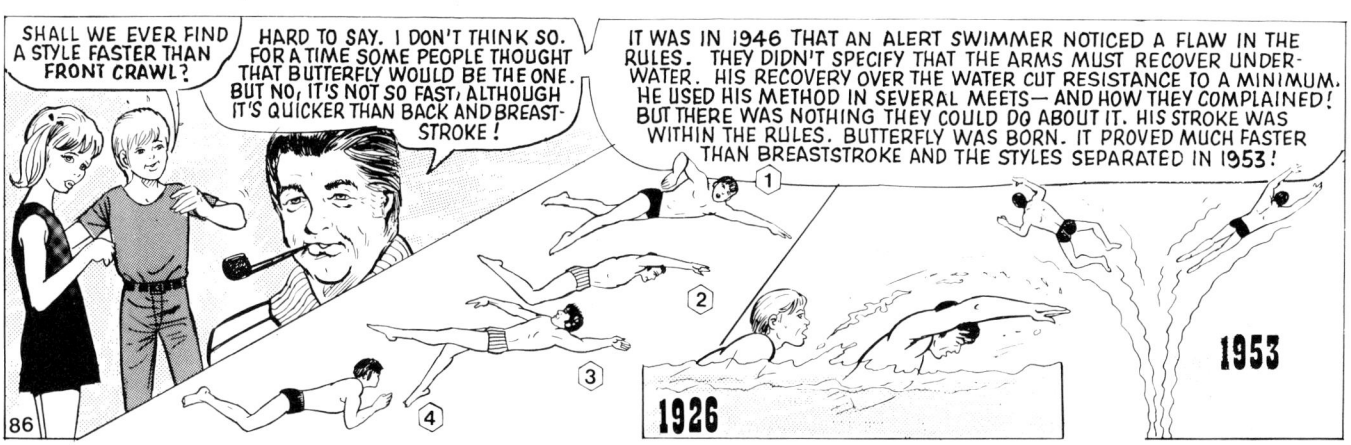

Derived activities

Why swim? Lots of reasons. There are all sorts of other sports that are open to swimmers: water polo surfing and diving to name but a few. There are many enjoyable social activities associated with swimming. And, as if any other explanation were needed, four fifths of good old Mother Earth is covered in water.

Try the diving board

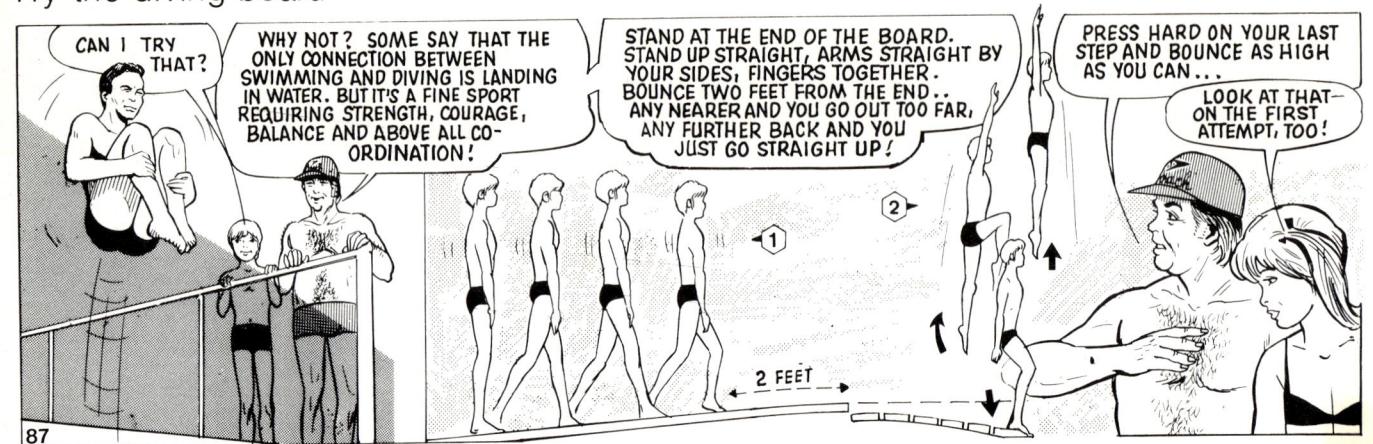

Straight, tucked, piked

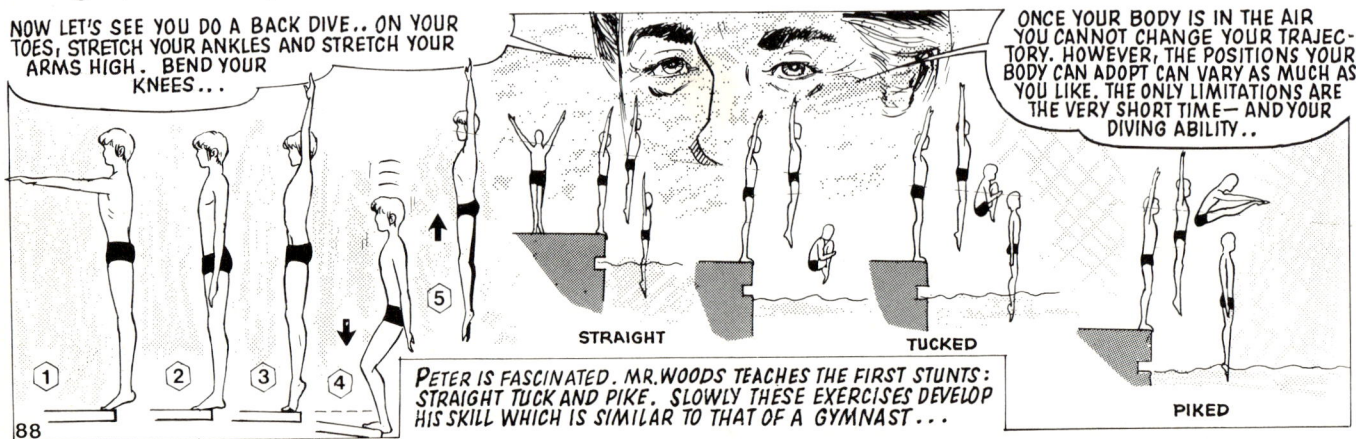

Variety in diving

Entry: beware of landing flat

Gymnastics for divers

A man's game

Water polo

Dribble, pass and shoot

A game of many facets

A sport for women

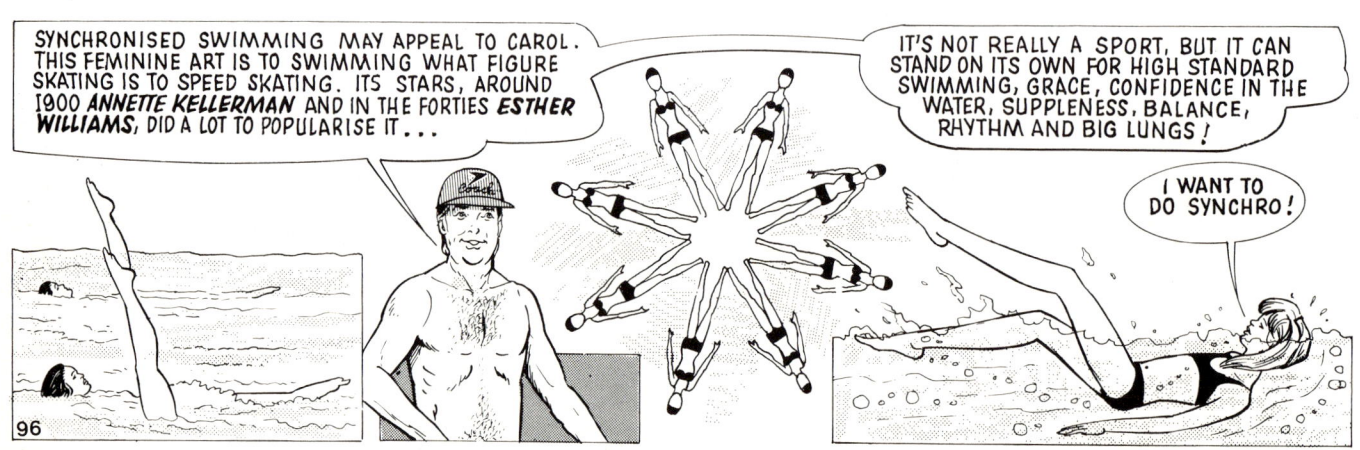

Figures and stunts

Swimming for all ages

Sub aqua

Long distance swimming

Swimming — new horizons

Great names in swimming history

1858
Jo Bennet (Sydney, Australia). Won the first so-called World Championship, held in Melbourne over 100 yards Freestyle.

1875
Captain Matthew Webb (Great Britain). Swam the Channel using Breaststroke.

1912
Duke Kahanamoku (Hawaiian Prince). Olympic 100 metres Freestyle winner 1912—1920. The greatest swimmer of the period.

1922
Johnny Weissmuller (USA, "Tarzan"). Undoubtedly the finest swimmer the world has known. Never beaten. Olympic champion 1924 and 1928.

1938—1954
Jack Hale (Hull, England). British champion and record holder of every Freestyle event over 200 metres. The war interrupted what would have been a fantastic career. The father of the dolphin kick in the Butterfly stroke and British champion in that stroke when over the age of 30.

1956—1964
Murray Rose (Australia). Olympic champion 400m, 1956 and 1960, and 1500m Freestyle 1956. The world's outstanding swimmer of the time.

1956—1964
Dawn Fraser (Australia). The first woman to break one minute for 100m Freestyle. Winner of 100m Freestyle in three Olympics, 1956, 1960 and 1964.

1964—1968
Don Schollander (USA). Olympic winner 100m and 400m Freestyle in 1964 and 200m Freestyle 1968.

1972
Mark Spitz (USA) Winner of seven Olympic gold medals — an all-time record.

1968—1972
Roland Matthes (DDR). The greatest Backstroker in the world. Olympic champion 1968 and 1972.

1972—1976
Kornelia Ender (DDR). Olympic champion 1976 100m, 200m Freestyle, 100m Butterfly.

1972—1976
David Wilkie (Great Britain). Olympic champion 1976 200m Breaststroke, silver medallist 100m Breaststroke. Silver medallist 1972 200m Breaststroke.

Swimming terms

Backstroke Flags Row of flags strung across a pool to warn backstrokers that the end of the pool is five metres away.
Drills Methods of developing strokes.
Freestyle Relays A relay of swimmers, all swimming Freestyle.
Heats Grouping of competitors for racing.
IM Individual Medley (one race using all four main strokes in the order, Butterfly, Backstroke, Breaststroke and Freestyle).
Kicking Practising with legs only.
Medley Relay A relay of swimmers using all four strokes — first: Backstroke; second: Breaststroke; third: Butterfly; fourth: Freestyle.
Meet Competition.
Nationals National swimming, diving and synchronised swimming Championships.
Pulling Practising with arms only.
Scratching Withdrawing from a race.
Seeding Arranging competitors in order of their speeds.
Spearhead Method of arranging swimmers in a race, with fastest seeded swimmer in the centre lane.
Squad or Team Group of swimmers who come together for training.
Starting Blocks Platform from which individuals start a race.
Synchro Synchronised swimming.

Swimming organisations

ASA	Amateur Swimming Association (English)
ESSA	English Schools' Swimming Association
FINA	Amateur International Swimming Federation
GBASA	Great Britain Amateur Swimming Association (England, Scotland and Wales)
ISTC	Institute of Swimming Teachers and Coaches
RLSS	Royal Life Saving Society
SASA, WAWA	Scottish and Welsh Amateur Swimming Association

Biography

Charlie Wilson. DLC. ASA Coach. has been involved with swimming ever since he could float. As a boy he trained with the great British champion, Jack Hale, in Hull. Now he is official coach to the England Squad, having been to the 1976 Montreal Olympics as coach to the British Swimming team, and the World Student Games in Moscow in 1973 as Team Manager. He has been a Great Britain Coach since 1970 and is also coach to the great names of British swimming — among them Brian Brinkley, Barry Prime and Christine Jarvis, all GB captains. His home base is Bedford, where he teaches at the Bedford Modern School and runs the Modernian Swimming Club, which is famous as a nursery of stars. The list of his other achievements is long — from the captaincy of the Loughborough College Water Polo team, to founder membership of the British Swimming Coaches Association, to membership of the Amateur Swimming Association Swimming Committee, and to being married with two daughters. who are both keen swimmers.

Photographs

Page 8
Brian Brinkley instructing a group of children at Bedford Modern School.

Page 11
French 100m and ex-European Freestyle champion, Rousseau, conducts a coaching session. (Photo: Presse Sport)

Page 14
Brian Brinkley, as always, putting maximum effort into a training swim. (Photo: Allsport, Tony Duffy)

Page 16
Melissa Belote, American Backstroke champion stretching the start. (Photo: Allsport, Tony Duffy)

Page 21
Backstrokers achieving maximum burst of speed at the start by a push and arm swing. (Photo: Allsport, Tony Duffy)

Page 24
Wendy Lee of Canada turns her head for a breath. (Photo: Allsport, Tony Duffy)

Page 26
Shane Gould (Australia). In 1973, at the age of 15, she held every Freestyle world record from 100m to 1500m. (Photo: Allsport, Tony Duffy)

Page 31
Jim Montgomery, first man under 50 seconds for 100m. (Photo: Allsport, Tony Duffy)

Page 34
Swimmers are like icebergs — it all happens underwater. Steve Genter, top US freestyler. (Photo: Allsport, Tony Duffy)

Page 37
One of the greatest of all Dutch swimmers, Enith Brigitta. (Photo: Allsport, Tony Duffy)

Page 43
Mark Spitz, the greatest swimmer of our time — nine Olympic gold medals — seven in Munich, 1972. (Photo: Presse Sport)

Page 47
Big John Naber, World Swimmer of the Year 1976, winner of four gold medals at the Montreal Olympics. (Photo: Allsport, Tony Duffy)

Page 51
Individual swimmers choose different starting techniques, giving each a different point of entry into the water. (Photo: Allsport, Tony Duffy)

Page 54
The grace and sparkle of swimming, illustrated by Canadian Breaststroker, Sylvie Deschamps. (Photo: Allsport, Tony Duffy)

Page 59
David Wilkie demonstrating the powerful leg action that made him 200m Breaststroke Olympic champion, 1976. (Photo: Allsport, Tony Duffy)

Page 62
Jenny Turrall of Australia cries after breaking the world 800m record in London, 1975. (Photo: Allsport, Tony Duffy)

Page 66
Relaxing and concentrating before the start. (Photo: Presse Sport)

Page 69
Nobutaka Taguchi, Japan's 1972 Olympic 100m Breaststroke champion — noted for an extremely narrow Breaststroke kick. (Photo: Allsport, Tony Duffy)

Page 70
Johnny Weissmuller, winner of five gold medals at the 1924 and 1928 Olympics, with his trainer from Chicago, William Bachrach. (Photo: Presse Sport)

Page 73
Probably the greatest woman swimmer in the world, Kornelia Ender — four gold and one silver medal at the Montreal Olympics, 1976. (Photo: Allsport, Tony Duffy)

Page 76
The power and aggression that wins the toughest game in the world — water polo. (Photo: Presse Sport)

Page 80
Helen Koppell, one of Britain's leading divers, in action at the Munich Olympics, 1972. (Photo: Allsport, Tony Duffy)

Page 83
The graceful forms of synchronised swimming belie the hours of practice necessary to co-ordinate such delicate movements in the water.